LAKELAND

LANDSCAPE OF IMAGINATION

To the Eyes of the Man of Imagination,
Nature is Imagination itself.
WILLIAM BLAKE

LAKELAND

LANDSCAPE OF IMAGINATION

GORDON STAINFORTH

CONSTABLE

LONDON

FIRST PUBLISHED IN GREAT BRITAIN 1992
BY CONSTABLE AND COMPANY LIMITED
3 THE LANCHESTERS, 162 FULHAM PALACE ROAD
LONDON W6 9ER

COPYRIGHT © GORDON STAINFORTH 1992
GORDON STAINFORTH HAS ASSERTED HIS MORAL RIGHTS
ISBN 0 09 471800 8

DESIGNED BY IVOR CLAYDON
SET IN MONOPHOTO CALEDONIA BY
SERVIS FILMSETTING LTD, MANCHESTER
COLOUR SEPARATIONS BY
HILO OFFSET LTD, COLCHESTER
PRINTED IN GREAT BRITAIN BY
CLAYS LTD, ST IVES PLC

A CIP CATALOGUE RECORD FOR THIS BOOK
IS AVAILABLE FROM THE BRITISH LIBRARY

HALF-TITLE
GLENCOYNE BROW, ULLSWATER.

TITLE
LANGDALE AT SUNSET, FROM TOM HEIGHTS.

CONTENTS
THE SCAFELLS FROM THE HEAD OF MOSEDALE.

CONTENTS

ACROSS CRINKLE CRAGS
TOWARDS PIKE OF BLISCO,
FROM BOWFELL.

A LANDSCAPE OF THE IMAGINATION

TAKING A FRESH LOOK

The Lake District is a landscape of contrasts – of tranquil lakes and gentle hills interspersed with savage crags and gills, of pastoral valleys flanked by desolate mountain sides. It could be said to be like a symphony, with both masculine and feminine subjects, and with the seasons providing the 'movements', and the weather, the tempi. L.J. Oppenheimer, one of the pioneer rock climbers at the end of the last century, said that it contains 'as many different types of beauty as it has valleys, and each type ever varying in mood. Time may perhaps, through the ruthless hand of man, wither certain charms; but, as was said about Cleopatra of old, custom can never stale its infinite variety.' There is no one, quintessential Lakeland 'scene'; it is ever changing and never quite how we expected it.

A cliché one hears about the Lake District with monotonous regularity is that it has been 'tamed', but this is invariably put about by those who have only explored it from the road, and then only very superficially. The truth (that I hope this book will bear witness to) is that there are large areas, not so far from the road, which are still very much in their natural, unspoiled state. Of course, it is true that large paths do 'tame' the mountains to a certain extent, but it should be pointed out that there have been paths through these mountains since the age of the dinosaurs – and that, anyway, there are still considerable expanses without any such paths. Further, one could ask what is meant by saying that a path 'tames' the mountainside. Does it do so any more than a dry stone wall, for example? A path is nothing more than a line of wear, which may or may not have been 'repaired' or strengthened. What it does do is *spoil* the mountainside – aesthetically, and even structurally, if the damage is allowed to get out of control. But the wild, raw elements – the basic topography and the weather – remain unchanged. *In the only sense that matters*, then, I would argue that the Lakeland mountains are as wild as they have ever been. Indeed – bearing in mind the long history of mining here, from prehistoric times right into the present century – they are in some ways actually wilder.

More than any other comparable beauty spot in the world, it is this corner of England that has captured the imagination of creative thinkers, writers and artists – many, such as Wordsworth, Coleridge, Southey, de Quincey, and Ruskin being literary figures of great importance. And, for all its familiarity, the Lakeland landscape still has enormous potential to capture our imagination today. Unfortunately, however, many come here – to use a very apt old Cumbrian expression – as true 'Off-comers', with no apparent wish to interact imaginatively or creatively with the landscape.

A PLACE OF STORYTELLING

My concern, then, is to get back to the unspoiled landscape, back to the hills, and to draw on some of the mystery that has been forgotten. First and foremost, we should consider the great enigma of its geological composition – an enormously slow process spread over hundreds of millions of years, that is many times more complex than we could imagine in our wildest dreams.

First, the whole area was submerged under an ocean which had many of the characteristics of the primal 'watery abyss' of mythology, containing among other things a stagnant black mud out of which the first forms of life developed. But the two opposing continental shore lines were closing fast – at the rate of two or three centimetres a year – and, when they collided, a vast mountain chain was thrown up. After another hundred million years these Himalayan-scale 'Caledonian Mountains' had been completely eroded away, and were covered by the sea once more. All the while, the whole land mass of the 'Eur-American continent' was drifting northwards through the climatic zones so that tropical seas gave way to equatorial swamps and, eventually, desert conditions, similar to those on the Arabian peninsula today. However, as it continued northwards, the land mass started to break up and the old Caledonian mountains reasserted themselves to stand high once more above the surrounding lowlands. Meanwhile, they had entered the Arctic zone ...

It is a fantastic story and hard to even *imagine*. There is little we can see with our eyes to suggest it, and because there is no way we can visualise the process through geological time, we are much more likely to regard it as something completed, as a sort of finished work of art that was always intended to look like this from the outset. That it was, in other words, created for *us*.

This ancient, primitive belief in an 'eternal' landscape which was created suddenly and cataclysmically 'in the beginning' is given further support when we learn that, despite the long and complicated history just outlined, the major land-forms of the Lake

District are primarily the result of two rather short-lived, freak events in its geological history: first, a massive set of volcanic eruptions about 460 million years ago, and then, much later, a major ice age, finishing a 'mere' ten thousand years ago. If we were to put this whole history on a 24-hour clock, it would be a bit like a series of multiple explosions about 19 hours ago sending up molten lava from the depths, followed by many hours of gentle abrasion and buckling and silting over, and then about two and a half minutes ago, a demented sculptor coming and attacking it from above with an ice-pick, before being overcome by overheating.

It is from this strange geological history that all the other extraordinary qualities of the Lake District emanate. It is a truly fabulous landscape, a place of storytelling that captures the child's imagination in us. Once we have seen it, dream-like images remain lodged for ever in our minds and play on our imagination; we become haunted, like Wordsworth, by 'huge and mighty forms, that do not live like living men', moving slowly through the mind.

THE POWER OF LANDSCAPE

It was this haunting, emotive quality that John Ruskin, the great art critic and landscape theorist who lived in the Lake District in the latter half of the last century, was referring to when he wrote of 'the *imagination* of the hills, colouring, with their far-away memories, every lowland stone and herb.' He specifically addressed himself to 'the essential connection' between human emotion and what he called 'the power of landscape' – by which he meant a 'mysterious sense of *unaccountable* life' in material nature itself, such as 'no mere reasoning can either induce or controvert.' Although he was the first to criticise those who spoke of nature as if it were alive in a human sense – especially if all the writer was doing was transferring his own emotions on to the landscape (the 'Pathetic Fallacy') – Ruskin insisted that even a quite barren, mountainous landscape such as the Lake District had 'an animation and pathos of *its own*, wholly irrespective of human presence or passion.' More than that, the entire surface of the earth was a 'living hieroglyph ... a thing with an inner language', all the manifestations of which had 'reference to the human intelligence that perceives them.' So striking was this quality of hills and mountains that Ruskin described them as 'centres of imaginative energy'. But it should be said that, for him, this imaginative energy was a two-way affair – that, without the human imagination being brought to bear on it, the landscape was dead: 'True desertness is not want of leaves, but of life. Where humanity is not, the best natural beauty is more than vain.'

When Ruskin speaks of the power of landscape, he is referring to an inner quality that is not in any sense related to its scale. 'To the rightly perceiving mind,' he says, 'there is the same infinity, the same majesty, the same power, the same unity, and the same perfection manifest in the casting of the clay as in the scattering of the cloud, in the mouldering of the dust as in the kindling of the day-star.' In the same way that William Blake could see the world in a grain of sand, Ruskin was concerned with 'the deep infinity of the thing itself.'

HARD TARN, RUTHWAITE COVE, GRISEDALE.

The Lake District is a prime example of a landscape whose 'power' is more to do with intricacy than with size. Though it is certainly laid out on a grand scale, one never feels overwhelmed by it. It is at once vast and intimate, so that, even when one is completely alone in it, it always has a remarkably 'homely' feel.

'In simple earnest,' the great Lakes poet, Samuel Taylor Coleridge wrote in 1803, 'I never find myself alone within the embracement of rocks and hills, ... but my spirit courses, drives and eddies, like a Leaf in Autumn: a wild activity, of thoughts, imaginations, feelings, and impulses of motion, rises up from within me ...' And, in a crucial later note, he said that certain aspects of the external world seemed to exist already in his imagination:

In looking at the objects of Nature while I am thinking ... I seem rather to be seeking, as it were *asking* for, a symbolic language for something within me that already and for ever exists, than observing anything new. Even when that latter is the case, yet still I have always an obscure feeling as if that new phenomenon were the dim awaking of a forgotten or hidden truth of my inner nature.

CRYSTAL GHOSTS

Some have claimed that the apparent close link between the external world and the imagination is the result of our all being part of One Mind, or Will – that the whole of nature is a vast work of the imagination of which we are just a small part. But such a grand, all-encompassing theory is so broad in its scope as to be virtually meaningless, and we may be inclined to ask why such a Supermind never *behaves* like One Mind, but is forever squabbling with itself.

Wordsworth was careful to avoid any such simple conflation of World and Mind, being content to say merely that they are 'exquisitely fitted' to one another:

How exquisitely the individual Mind
... to the external World
Is fitted: – and how exquisitely, too –
Theme this but little heard of among men –
The external World is fitted to the Mind

Coleridge went a step further. While he agreed that the World and man are not One *Mind*, he insisted that we are all nonetheless part of one organism: 'Every Thing has a Life of its own, & we are all *one Life*,' he wrote. One hundred and eighty years before his time, Coleridge was subscribing to the 'Gaia theory' (named after the Greek goddess of the earth) which regards the whole planet as a single living organism.

Ruskin later took up the same theme with enthusiasm. In answer to the extraordinary question 'Are mountains alive?' – in a bizarre dialogue called '*The Ethics of the Dust*' – he retorted: 'Things are not either wholly alive, or wholly dead. They are less or more alive.' And, in keeping with his strongly held belief that everything in nature 'bears evidence of having been produced by the power of the same spirit as our own', he said that this life force was present 'wherever the dust of the earth begins to assume any orderly and lovely state.'

Crystals, for example, he described as having power, and 'breathing' – and, in short, as being subject to exactly the same creative and destructive forces as ourselves. In his eccentric way, Ruskin saw the 'life of crystals' and human life as having much in common:

> . . . you see the broad shadow and deadly force of inevitable fate . . . you see the multitudes of crystals whose time has come; not a set time, as with us, but yet a time, sooner or later, when they all must give up their crystal ghosts; – when the strength by which they grew, and the strength given them to breathe, pass away from them; and they fail, and are consumed, and vanish away: and another generation is brought to life, framed out of their ashes.

As so often in Ruskin's writing, the metaphor has become more important than the thing he is describing. He is clearly here at least as interested in human life, and *the way it is analogous to the life of crystals*, as he is in the life of crystals themselves.

FLUORITE, SPHALERITE, GALENA AND CALCITE CRYSTALS, FROM RUSKIN'S COLLECTION.

You may look at them, once understanding their fate, with endless interest. You will see crowds of unfortunate little crystals, who have been forced to constitute themselves in a hurry; you will see them doing their best, bright and numberless, but tiny. And you will see deceitful crystals, that look soft as velvet, and are deadly to all near them. And sometimes you will see fat crystals eating up thin ones, like great capitalists and little labourers; and politico-economic crystals teaching the stupid ones how to eat each other, and cheat each other; and foolish crystals getting in the way of wise ones; and impatient crystals spoiling the plans of patient ones, irreparably; just as things go on in the world.

JOHN RUSKIN

'A SON OF THE EARTH'

Where Coleridge differed from Ruskin was in not being content with keeping this theoretical link between the landscape and man simply at a theoretical level; for him, the Oneness was something that had to be experienced. He had to put 'the power of landscape' to the test by going off into the wilds.

So it was that, on 1st August 1802, Coleridge set out with just a stick and a knapsack (made from an old piece of 'natty green oilskin') on what he called a 'circumcursion' of the central fells. 'In spite of Mrs. C and Mary, who both raised their voices against it, ... off I sallied.'

Once he was in the mountains, Coleridge was in his element, for he had long regarded himself as 'a detached individual, a *Terrae Filius*' (a 'son of the Earth'):

The farther I ascend from animated Nature, from men, and cattle, and the common birds of the woods, and fields, the greater becomes in me the Intensity of the feeling of Life. Life seems to me then a universal spirit, that neither has, nor can have, an opposite. ...

The 5th August saw Coleridge making an ascent of Scafell. At the summit, he was astounded by the new world that opened up before him:

O my God! what enormous Mountains these are close by me, and yet below the Hill I stand on – Great Gavel, Kirk Fell, Green Crag, and behind the Pillar, then the Steeple, then the Haycock. ... But O! what a look down just under my Feet! The frightfullest Cove that might ever be seen, huge perpendicular Precipices, and one Sheep upon it's only Ledge, that surely must be crag! ... I must now drop down, how I may into Eskdale.

And this was where his problems began, especially as, on his own admission, he was always 'too confident and too indolent to look round about and wind about 'till I find a track or other symptom of safety.' It was a 'sort of Gambling', he said, to which he was addicted: 'I wander on, and where it is first *possible* to descend, there I go – relying upon fortune for how far down this possibility will continue.' And so it was that he found himself making the first recorded descent of Broad Stand, which is quite justifiably still given the rock-climbing grade of Difficult. After a hair-raising time negotiating a series of vertical steps, and believing himself to be past the main difficulties (he wasn't!), he calmed down a bit. He found himself quite suddenly 'in a state of almost prophetic Trance & Delight', and he 'blessed God aloud, for the powers of Reason & the Will, which remaining, no Danger can overpower us! O God, I exclaimed aloud – how calm, how blessed am I now: I know not how to proceed, how to return; but I am calm & fearless & confident.'

Coleridge was in fact experiencing something that all climbers and explorers have experienced in difficult situations – an extraordinary dual state in which wild excitement is balanced by calm reason, in which one is super-alert yet relaxed at the same time.

OFF THE BEATEN TRACK

In the Lake District today, solo climbing or bivouacking high in the mountains is about the only means still open to us of experiencing the wild landscape on this one-to-one basis. Only in this way can we confront the raw elements and have a sight, in Wordsworth's words, of 'that immortal sea Which brought us hither'. Life is reduced to its bare essentials, and any fanciful 'armchair' notions of wilderness are replaced by hard realities that are stripped of any wrappings. We have put ourselves in the state that was simply and eloquently summed up by the Chinese mystic Lao Tzu, in the fifth century B.C.:

Blank as a piece of uncarved wood;
Yet receptive as a hollow in the hills.

The walker who enters the mountain landscape in this spirit is quiet and receptive, appreciative of all the signs of nature and of being a part of nature. In a sense, the object is to *disappear* into the landscape, to become one with it; one has no wish to draw attention to oneself, or to leave signs of one's being there.

This whole approach to living and walking in the hills is completely opposed to the modern mania for following named and beaten paths – of thoughtlessly, ritualistically, fervently, wearing and deepening existing grooves. Of course, where there is serious damage, and the route is a popular one, there is no other solution but to repair the path and encourage walkers to stick to it. Fortunately, in the Lake District, this essential repair work, which is carried out by the National Trust, is based on a sound philosophy of minimising the impact on the landscape. To this end, all footpath repair now uses an ancient technique known as 'pitching' in which giant cobblestones of native rock are embedded deep into the hill side, rather like a dry stone wall tipped on its side and sunk into the ground. This method, which was used for

LIGHTWEIGHT TENT IN GREAT MOSS, UPPER ESKDALE.

HELL GILL, LANGDALE.

many centuries, at least since Roman times, but was not re-discovered until the mid-1980s, has been found to be far more durable than any modern technique, as well as being aesthetically pleasing and requiring virtually no maintenance.

Often, where the path is very severely damaged, it has to be re-directed, and here a great deal of thought has to be put into the route it takes to ensure that it blends as much as possible with the surroundings, twisting and turning in harmony with the natural features. The path builders are purists: all the work is done by hand, and only indigenous materials are used. And they are real enthusiasts: only those with a genuine empathy for the wild landscape (generally climbers and walkers) are allowed to work on the teams.

For the most frequented routes in the mountains this new, 'purist' technique is obviously a very encouraging development. But it can never address the whole problem, for a lot of the damage is, I believe, totally unnecessary. There is a type of walker who will apparently stick to any path, come what may, even when it has not been repaired and is in a very severely eroded condition. A worn and broken path such as that beside Hell Gill in Langdale, for example (page 15), seems to act like a magnet to a certain type of 'achievement-hungry', 'experience-consuming' tourist. Because others – many others – have gone that way they feel compelled to do so as well, irrespective of the damage it might cause.

This type of massive scar is to me a painful lesion, and for walkers to follow it blindly, contributing to its already hopelessly torn surface, is like the wilful scratching of an open wound. And the irony is that very often, just next to these hideous, loose paths, there are superb, easy scrambling routes on perfect rock. (The most popular routes up Bowfell and Wetherlam are good examples: both of these can be avoided by scrambling routes just to one side which go virtually the whole way to the summit without touching either grass or detritus.)

Where a path is damaged it is probably better to ignore it and take a completely different route where there is no damage and where one is in no danger of doing any. Indeed, more and more it is my strategy not to follow conventional footpaths at all, but to make my own way. More and more, I am inclined to say, with Coleridge: 'Every man his own path-maker'.

PITCHED FOOTPATH NEAR
DUNGEON GHYLL, LANGDALE.

UNIQUE AND UNTRACEABLE

But there is one overriding principle which must be constantly borne in mind when going 'off-route', and that is that we should leave everything exactly as we found it. Let it become the norm, the rule, of all hill-walking that we never leave any trace of our passing, whether it be in the form of litter or footprints; and let us regard any mark we leave as a mark of failure. To put it even more strongly, I would say that any such mark removes our right to be there. This may sound like an unrealistic ideal, but I can honestly say that, in the four months I spent in the Lake District for the main shoot of this book, once I was away from the valley floor I rarely touched a path and scarcely left a single footprint. Moving across the terrain in this way is an absorbing exercise that adds considerably to the enjoyment of a walk, transforming it, as it does, from a trudge into a craft.

I have two other 'rules', both of a much less serious nature (– rules to be broken!). The first is, generally to avoid repeating a route, even if it is one of my own invention. A great mountain day is not something that can be repeated anyway; or rather, its repeatability is inversely proportional to its greatness. Better not to attempt it, better by far to set out on new adventures. At the simplest level, this means: every time a new route. Let every route, every excursion, be unique and of the moment; not another person's, not a repeat of one's own.

My second preference, amounting almost to a rule, is to walk in the mountains only in very small parties or on my own. Large parties are contrary to my whole way of thinking. They contribute most of all to worn paths; they inhibit individual spontaneity and the scope for adventure; and they limit the participants' ability to appreciate their surroundings. A large party dilutes the experience both for its own members and for others in the vicinity: it encroaches on other people's space. Generally, the interests which a large party has in the hills are totally different from that of a solo walker. The landscape is no longer of central importance to the day.

'SAUNTERING'

'Sallying forth' into the mountains is a very personal experience, and only by doing so alone can one experience the world (and oneself), as Coleridge did, directly and truly – without any protective masks, or social posturing of any kind. The interaction of people has no bearing whatever on a mountain landscape. Hill walking in its purest form is about individual poetry, not group drama or self-promotion in a group.

Exploring the landscape imaginatively means, above all, having a 'passion', like Wordsworth, for wandering, and a dislike for following straight paths which reduce mountain days to a mere routine of going from A to B and back again (for the climber, this is typically: A for Automobile, B for the final Belay at the top of the climb, and C – less frequently – the ritual walk to the summit Cairn). The kind of route I am advocating is circular: it goes from A to X (which is preferably somewhere *other* than the obvious B) and back to A again, without going over any of the same ground twice.

The creative spirit is one that prefers arcs and circles to straight lines, for they are the way to unforeseen possibilities. This is the spirit of the great Lakeland conservationist of the 1930s, the Reverend H.H.Symonds, who hankered for 'old-fashioned, skimble-skamble, bandy-legged divergences which took us as the spirit moved or the slope invited.'

Such spontaneity always implies a certain lunacy, boldness, and even a touch of incompetence. It is epitomised by J. Menlove Edwards' first 'free' (unaided), on-sight lead of the Great Flake on the Central Buttress of Scafell in 1931. The second man in the party described the scene:

> In my haste to catch up with the others, I had left my rubbers behind and was climbing in stockinged feet. At the foot of the Flake, Menlove quickly arranged some slings and brought me up to him. Our whole performance was hair-raisingly chaotic. For some reason I was still carrying the spare line. I gripped hold of Menlove's shoulders and we both swung out from the rock. He seemed to be only very loosely tied in. My strength was by then running out. I seized hold of a spare rope which Menlove had secured to the chockstone and lowered myself until I could jam my body into the crack and take a rest. Menlove meanwhile was making fresh arrangements with the rope. Suddenly he called out: 'I'm going to have a go!' Next moment he was laybacking steadily up the crack, unbelayed, and was soon at the top.

Of course, although it *looks* very chaotic, this kind of adventurous spontaneity is based on a shrewd assessment of all the factors involved – for only a very fine sense of judgement can turn a crazy hunch into a reality, as Edwards so brilliantly did here.

In considering the whole process of creative divergences from the beaten track, I am reminded of the great nineteenth century American writer, Henry David Thoreau, and his concept of 'sauntering'. This is a kind of imaginative wandering that has an underlying sense of purpose to it, albeit at times an unconscious one. The saunterer is never a mere idler or vagabond. 'The

saunterer, in the good sense,' says Thoreau, 'is no more vagrant
than the meandering river, which is all the while sedulously
seeking the shortest course to the sea.' He is not a Knight, but a
'Walker, Errant'. Sauntering is always *deliberate* – deliberate in its
initial intention and deliberate in the way it is pursued (a continual
weighing-up, poised in balance on a knife-edge, as it were,
between the known and the unknown) – but the line of the route is
never totally predictable. Nevertheless, Thoreau had an
unshakeable belief in 'a subtle magnetism in Nature, which, if we
unconsciously yield to it, will direct us aright'.

'Sauntering' is a kind of *unravelling*, a journey that links with
our inner, imaginative landscape and so becomes, in a very real
sense, a journey into our true selves. In Thoreau's words, what we
are trying to do is 'take that walk, never yet taken by us through
this actual world, which is perfectly symbolic of the path which we
love to travel in the interior and ideal world . . .'

'A SPIRITUAL MAP WITH OUR TRACKS'

Sauntering in Thoreau's sense is a very creative use of the landscape: by following our hunches, we 'home' in on something deep in ourselves. The distinction between the external landscape we perceive and the internal landscape of our imagination starts to break down. The former always involves the latter to some extent anyway, whether we care to admit it or not. The choice of what parts of it we inhabit or explore, and our understanding of what we choose to notice in it, is the very framework of the landscape for us. This framework *is* our landscape.

Likewise, in the photography for this book, I have certainly been highly selective, and have undoubtedly to some extent created or recreated the Lake District as I imagine it. What I have done in a minor way, is what imaginative minds like Beatrix Potter and Arthur Ransome have done in a much more extreme way, when the real Lakeland landscape has been completely reconstructed into a 'lakeland of the imagination'. In Arthur Ransome, for example, Lake Windermere and Coniston Water become one – it is just 'the lake', a total amalgam of childhood fantasy and reality. The landscape is no longer neutral, or 'innocent', but highly personal; it contains part of the artist's 'life story'.

In a superbly rich and suggestive metaphor, the Lakes poet Thomas de Quincey compares the human brain with a *palimpsest* – an ancient manuscript on which successive layers have been erased to make way for later pieces of writing. The hidden layers correspond to the recoverable deposits of memory lying below the surface of consciousness:

> What else than a natural and mighty palimpsest is the human brain? ... Everlasting layers of ideas, images, feelings, have fallen upon your brain softly as light. Each succession has seemed to bury all that went before. And yet in reality not one has been extinguished. ... The fleeting accidents of a man's life, and its external shows, may indeed be irrelate and incongruous; but the organising principles which fuse into harmony, and gather about fixed predetermined centres, whatever heterogeneous elements life may have accumulated from without, will not permit the grandeur of human unity greatly to be violated ...

I would now like to borrow this idea from de Quincey and use it in a slightly different way by suggesting that the personal landscape 'map', or picture of the real landscape which we build up and store in our mind, is just such a palimpsest: it is a dynamic, imaginative creation in which a complex series of wandering 'excursions' and adventures is inscribed successively onto a 'vast' inner map, to form a matrix of successive layers, a patchwork of intertwining journey-lines, a web of criss-crossing memory beads that are interconnected only by our intuition and imagination. In the words of Coleridge, it is a 'spiritual map, with our tracks'.

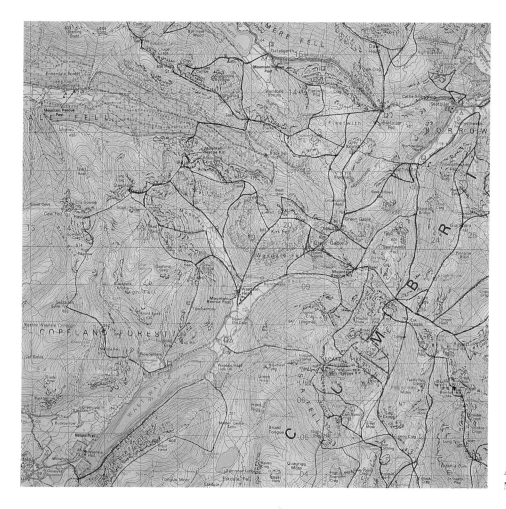

A LAKELAND ENTHUSIAST'S MAP OF THE CENTRAL FELLS.

The operation of the imagination in this way is not a 'mode of behaviour' that we can drop in and out of, like a hobby or pastime, but an ongoing process that is central to life. 'The imagination is not a State,' William Blake once said: 'it is the Human existence itself.'

This indeed was one of my first and clearest realisations about mountain walking and climbing, right from the day I first discovered it – that, as an activity, it was not peripheral, but was somehow central to life, and would always remain so. That it was, as it were, a condition of life, *for* life. 'There arises a consciousness of momentum,' the Victorian mountaineer, Sir Martin Conway, said. 'On and on one must go. It is like life.' And, like a palimpsest, each stage in the journey somehow *grows out of* and contains all that has gone before – even if much of it has apparently been forgotten. Dorothy Pilley, a great woman climber of the 1920s, said it goes right down into the 'very form and fabric' of oneself.

Although the 'map' is never finished, there are nevertheless days when a whole 'leg' of the journey seems to have been completed – a 'day of days' which is somehow a culmination of all the previous days in that landscape. After which we can only move on in a completely different direction.

OVER THE HILLS AND FAR AWAY

In a sense, a mountain skyline, like the horizon, represents a boundary between the intellect and the imagination, for it is impossible to say without prior knowledge what lies on the other side. When we head into the hills, it is not just a fascination for the topography (topophilia), and the intellectual and physical puzzle of how it fits together, that draws us on. We want to see what lies *beyond*, what new world opens up. We want to walk right up to, and across, the boundaries of our dreams. 'Over the hills' there is a world where fantasy and reality merge.

In Beatrix Potter's '*Tale of Pigling Bland*', the concept of going 'over the hills' is closely linked to that of 'finding one's way home' – 'over the hills and far away' from the 'grown-up' world of commerce and dull-witted regulations, finding one's way 'home' . . . to one's real self. It is all about making crucial choices about where and how one is going to live. Where one is going to live, metaphorically.

I may be accused of reading too much into it, but it seems to me that, like many of Beatrix Potter's 'little books', this tale contains worlds of meaning. Major universal themes are hinted at in the most subtle way. (They are never more than hinted at.) There is always a sense of a larger story concerning the natural order of things – a harsh world that is full of contradictions and unfathomable mysteries. There is also an acute awareness of the *paradoxes* of nature – that it has a dark as well as a light side. And, as in any great fairy tale or myth, the basic elements are set out with beautiful economy and clarity. 'Home' is represented by Westmorland; commerce and the market place, by Lancashire; the boundary between them, by the River Brathay, and the means of crossing it, Colwith Bridge.

The Market is established from the outset as being something very serious that overshadows the whole of life – for all practical purposes, Fate itself, the fate of being this particular animal (the fate of pigs being to lead 'prosperous, uneventful lives', i.e. get fat! but – as Pig-wig herself remarks, 'cheerfully' – to end up as 'Bacon, hams'.)

Yet free will can still be exercised.

'Why on earth don't you run away?' exclaimed the horrified Pigling.
'I shall after supper,' said Pig-wig decidedly.

However, it is not as simple as that; it is not so easy to escape the food chain! Escape is only possible with vision and imagination. It is not just a simple choice between stark polarities: there is often a third way, which involves lateral thinking and cunning. It is symbolised in the tale by the important image of the three-way signpost. Straight ahead (the way Pigling has been told to go) leads 'To Market Town', while to one side, and far less obviously, is the way 'Over the hills'. Only once Pigling has become hopelessly lost in a dark wood does the opportunity present itself for him to escape 'Over the hills'. From then on, it is largely a matter of being quick-witted, sharp-eyed, and deceptive.

Pigling and Pig-wig's final escape over the bridge, to dance 'over the hills and far away', represents the rather wistful ideal of the triumph of the spirit of childhood innocence over the insensitive boorishness of the 'adult' world – a world of authority and 'pig licences', and the total, unquestioning acceptance of the law of the 'market'. It is idealistic because it rules out the possibility of compromise, of living with one foot in each world. Beatrix Potter, who actually writes herself into the beginning of the story, warns the characters directly: 'Remember, if you once cross the county boundary you cannot come back'.

Everyone is faced with a crossroads, and a dark wood; the question is, have we the imagination and initiative to cross the bridge? Or, are we stuck in our own very worn groove?

THE FLATLAND

Beatrix Potter's 'Westmorland', standing as it does for the 'freedom of the hills' in contrast with the all-pervading 'law' of the Market in Lancashire, could be said to have something in common with Thomas Mann's *The Magic Mountain*, of which Joseph Campbell has written:

The call to adventure is to a land of no return that is absolutely removed from every law and notion of the 'flatland' (as Mann calls it): the business-land, the newspaper-and-ledger-land, of the hero's native city . . . On the flatland life is reaction, whereas on the timeless mountaintop . . . there can be fermentation, spontaneity, action as opposed to reaction.

Today the gap between the flatland and the hills is as wide as ever, seeing that we are out of touch with the natural world to a more serious, *less excusable*, extent than ever before in our history. We appear to be caught up in an ever deepening vortex of growth economics and mass entertainment in which wild places run the risk of being turned into theme parks, and the flatland approximates more and more the dim, vicarious world of 'virtual reality'.

'Whither is fled the visionary gleam?' Wordsworth demanded in 1804: 'Where is it now, the glory and the dream?' He saw the problem very much in terms of the adult losing the fresh receptivity of the child and, in effect, falling asleep. In some of his most famous lines he wrote:

> Our birth is but a sleep and a forgetting:
> ... Shades of the prison-house begin to close
>   Upon the growing boy,

and he concluded that we act as if our 'whole vocation were endless imitation'.

Coleridge put it in even stronger terms when he spoke of the spirit that has become 'denaturalised'. He described such a person – he was referring to William Pitt! – as

> A plant sown and reared in a hot house, for whom the very air, that surrounded him, had been regulated by the thermometer of previous purpose; to whom the light of nature had penetrated only through glasses and covers; who had had the sun without the breeze; whom no storm had shaken; on whom no rain had pattered; on whom the dews of Heaven had not fallen!'

Many people who visit the Lake District today are so 'denaturalised in spirit' that they remain essentially *detached* from the landscape, and are crippled by what I can only describe as geomorphological blindness. For example, many who walk up Scafell Pike seem scarcely to notice the finest piece of rock architecture in England, Scafell Crag, just opposite them. The reason, it seems, is that they have not been *told* to notice it – it has not been labelled as a 'sight' to be seen – such as Aira Force or Friar's Crag.

FOR THE FREE SPIRIT

As an unspoiled landscape, which is nothing less than a gigantic work of art, the Lake District demands an imaginative response that does not, however, mark or damage it in any way. This is the challenge that it throws out to us. It was Percy Unna who said, in his famous 'guidelines' of 1937 (which are still held as sacrosanct by the National Trust today), that the land must 'be maintained in its primitive condition for all time with unrestricted access to the public'. Unna then went on to spell out very precisely what he meant by this – his two most important provisos being:

> That 'Primitive' means not less primitive than the existing state.
> That the hills should not be made easier or safer to climb.

Unna would have unquestionably agreed with Thoreau's great dictum: 'In Wildness is the preservation of the World'.

The spirit that does not want to be tamed does not want the landscape to be tamed. If we tame, prettify, or commercialise it, we shall paradoxically turn it into a wasteland, a fossilised relic that has lost all its potential as an arena in which the imaginative spirit can flourish. That is how I see the Lake District – as a landscape for the imaginative Free Spirit which is in essential harmony with nature, and is entirely at odds with the conformism of organised routes and the march of 'market forces'. The pathway of the free spirit does not lead to the market.

Only in such an unspoiled landscape can the whole person – physical, intellectual, and imaginative – flourish. Only here will our personal 'inner maps' continue to grow and develop. In this way, our perception of the landscape will never remain static, but will be ever richer and more surprising. It may well be that we shall make the mistake one day of believing that our personal map of it is complete, and that the landscape itself thus has little more to offer – that, in common parlance, we have 'done' it. Only later shall we realise just how inadequate our appreciation of it first was, as whole new worlds open up, far greater and richer than any we had previously imagined – or had been able to imagine, so limited and undeveloped were our creative powers in our earlier days.

A CABINET OF BEAUTIES

In Cumberland and Westmorland there is a cabinet of beauties, – each thing being beautiful in itself, and the very passage of one lake, mountain or valley, to another, is itself a beautiful thing again.

S.T. COLERIDGE

A PEACEFUL MAY EVENING IN GRISEDALE.

RYDAL WATER ON AN EARLY
MORNING IN SPRING. A FEW
HUNDRED YARDS FROM WHERE
THIS PICTURE WAS TAKEN IS
NAB COTTAGE, THE HOME OF
THOMAS DE QUINCEY, AND
LATER, OF COLERIDGE'S SON,
HARTLEY.

ACROSS LOUGHRIGG TOWARDS
HELVELLYN FROM BLACK FELL.

BIRCH TREES ON KING'S HOW, BORROWDALE.

DESCENDING INTO TROUTDALE
FROM GRANGE FELL ON A WARM
SPRING EVENING.

TROUTDALE AND BLACK CRAG,
BORROWDALE.

THE 'JAWS OF BORROWDALE'
FROM MAIDEN MOOR.

THIRLMERE AND HAWES HOW
ISLAND FROM THE RAVINE OF
LAUNCHY GILL.

ENNERDALE WATER, FROM
BOWNESS KNOTT.

A LONG WAY HOME: STYHEAD
TARN AND DISTANT
BORROWDALE FROM LINGMELL
COL, LATE EVENING.

LATE WINTER SNOW ON STONY
COVE PIKE ABOVE PATTERDALE.

ROCK ART

The work of the Great Spirit of nature is as deep and unapproachable in the lowest as in the noblest objects – the Divine mind is as visible in its full energy of operation on every lowly bank and mouldering stone, as in the lifting of the pillars of heaven, and settling the foundation of the earth; and to the rightly perceiving mind, there is the same infinity, the same majesty, the same power, the same unity, and the same perfection, manifest in the casting of the clay as in the scattering of the cloud, in the mouldering of the dust as in the kindling of the day-star.

JOHN RUSKIN, 1843

LICHEN ON CAT BELLS, BORROWDALE

QUARTZ-TOPAZ GREISEN ON
WATER CRAG NEAR DEVOKE
WATER.

SUMMIT BOULDER ON
LINGMELL, ABOVE WASDALE
HEAD.

'PAINTED WALL', CASTLE CRAG,
BORROWDALE.

BRECCIATED OUTCROP ON
MAIDEN MOOR, HIGH ABOVE
DERWENT WATER.

CAVE CEILING, CASTLE CRAG,
BORROWDALE.

NATURAL 'LITHOCHROMY'–
THE ART OF PAINTING ON
STONE – CASTLE CRAG.

NATURE SHEDS A TEAR ON THE
'PAINTED WALL', CASTLE CRAG.

GORSE ON CATBELLS,
BORROWDALE.

STILL WILD

*I now entered Westmorland, a
county eminent only for being the
wildest, most barren, and frightful
of any that I have passed over in
England and Wales. The west side,
which borders on Cumberland, is
indeed bounded by a chain of
almost unpassable Mountains,
which in the language of the
country are called Fells ...*

DANIEL DEFOE, 1724

THE REMOTE HEART OF THE CENTRAL FELLS: THE SCAFELL PIKES AS SEEN FROM GREY FRIAR.

LOOKING DOWN ON THE
DESOLATE UPPER END OF
DEEPDALE FROM GREENHOW
END.

BARREN ROCKSCAPE ON
BOWFELL: PIKE OF STICKLE
FROM FLAT CRAGS.

ESKDALE FELL AND ESK PIKE
ON A FINE SPRING EVENING.

ACROSS BLIND TARN,
MITERDALEHEAD MOSS, TO
ULPHA FELL.

VIEW OUT TOWARDS THE IRISH
SEA FROM BLEA TARN.

BLEA TARN ABOVE ESKDALE,
WITH GREEN CRAG BEHIND.

THE FORMIDABLE GREAT
GULLY OF WASTWATER SCREES.

*Scale-Force Waterfall is 200 feet
perpendicular, except where it
flushes over a small jut; the steep
on both sides is covered with
variety of moss, fern, ash and oak,
all fed by the constant spray and
flourish in indescribable verdure
… Although you may be wet with
the spray, you cannot help feeling
the solemnity of this deep, this
musical abyss, enchanting as
verdure and melody can make it.*
CAPTAIN JOSEPH BUDWORTH, 1792

SCALE FORCE, THE HIGHEST
WATERFALL IN THE LAKE
DISTRICT.

WINTER

*There is hardly any time of year at
which a trip to Lakeland is more
thoroughly enjoyable. How
different are the firm outlines of
those distant peaks from the hazy
indistinctness which usually falls to
the lot of the summer tourist!
What sensation is more delightful
than that of tramping along while
the crisp snow crunches under
foot, and gazing upward at the
lean black crags standing boldly
out from the long smooth slopes of
dazzling white!*

W.P. HASKETT SMITH, 1894

ALPINE CONDITIONS ON THE EAST FACE OF ILL CRAG, SCAFELL PIKE.

(PAGE 60/61) ST SUNDAY CRAG
AND DEEPDALE FROM THE
SUMMIT OF FAIRFIELD AFTER
AN APRIL BLIZZARD.

ICE ENCRUSTED BOULDERS
ABOVE THE KIRKSTONE PASS.

SUMMIT CAIRN ON CAUDALE
MOOR IN FEBRUARY.

(PAGE 60/61) ST SUNDAY CRAG
AND DEEPDALE FROM THE
SUMMIT OF FAIRFIELD AFTER
AN APRIL BLIZZARD.

ICE ENCRUSTED BOULDERS
ABOVE THE KIRKSTONE PASS.

ON THE KIRKSTONE ROAD
ABOVE STOCK GHYLL BEFORE
DAWN.

THE SAME, AT DAWN.

LIGHT AND SHADE ON THE
EASTERN COVES OF HELVELLYN
AFTER A SNOW STORM.

Along the brink
Of Russet Cove, and those two other Coves,
Huge skeletons of crags, which form the trunk
Of old Helvellyn spread their arms abroad,
And make a stormy harbour for the winds.
WILLIAM WORDSWORTH, 1805

ACROSS THE GREAT RIDGES OF
DOVEDALE AND DEEPDALE TO
HELVELLYN FROM CAUDALE
MOOR.

HELVELLYN FROM FAIRFIELD
IN WINTER.

*Near that very Tarn William and I
bade him [Wordsworth's brother
John] farewell the last time he was
at Grasmere, when he went from
us to take the command of the
ship. We were in view of the head
of Ulswater, and stood till we
could see him no longer, watching
him as he hurried down the stony
mountain. Oh! my dear Friend,
you will not wonder that we love
that place. I have been twice to it
since his death.*
DOROTHY WORDSWORTH, 1805

GRISEDALE TARN FROM
DEEPDALE HAUSE.

ON THE SUMMIT OF GREAT
GABLE IN NOVEMBER.

DOLLYWAGGON PIKE AND
FALCON CRAG IN THE GRIP OF
WINTER ICE.

One travels along with the lines of a mountain. Years ago I wanted to make Wordsworth sensible of this .... Would I repose, my soul lies and is quiet upon the broad level vale. Would it act? it darts up into the mountain-top like a kite, and like a chamois-goat runs along the ridge – or like a boy that makes a sport on the road of running along a wall or narrow fence!

S.T. COLERIDGE, 1804

SHARP EDGE, BLENCATHRA,
EARLY APRIL.

HIGH ON GRASMOOR ON A WILD
EVENING IN FEBRUARY.

WILD DAYS IN UPPER ESKDALE

Hence upwards, Eskdale is a glorious wilderness. Dungeon Gill and Wasdale-head Hotels are the nearest houses, five miles as the crow flies, but with Bowfell in the way of the one and Scafell in the way of the other. You can play at being lost, and imagine a great lone land. We have no other bit of wild country like this, and hitherto it has not been spoiled for the purposes of a playground by too much meddling. A very little pathmaking and setting up of signposts would take away the charm of finding your own road, of attacking Nature single-handed, which is the thing that gives our homeland an advantage over more stupendous Alps.

W.G. COLLINGWOOD, 1902

SCAFELL PIKE FROM THE HEAD OF MOSEDALE.

THE SCAFELL PIKES FROM
GREAT MOSS.

SCAFELL PIKE AND ESK
BUTTRESS FROM THE EDGE OF
GREAT MOSS.

*My mind feels as if it ached to behold and know something
great – something one and indivisible – and it is only in
the faith of this that rocks or waterfalls, mountains or
caverns give me the sense of sublimity or majesty!*
S.T. COLERIDGE, 1797

COLERIDGE'S DESCENT ROUTE
FROM SCAFELL IN 1802: BROAD
STAND, MICKLEDORE AND CAM
SPOUT.

OFF THE BEATEN TRACK IN
UPPER ESKDALE IN MARCH.

O God! what thoughts were mine!
O how I wished for Health and
Strength that I might wander
about for a Month together, in the
stormiest month of the year,
among these Places, so lonely and
savage and full of sounds!

S.T. COLERIDGE, 1802

OMINOUS CLOUDS GATHER
OVER SCAFELL AND GREAT
MOSS.

ON HIGH GAIT CRAGS IN
THREATENING WEATHER
CONDITIONS.

How divine,
The liberty, for frail, for mortal, man
To roam at large among unpeopled glens
And mountainous retirements, only trod
By devious footsteps; regions consecrate
To oldest time! and, reckless of the storm
That keeps the raven quiet in her nest,
Be as a presence or a motion – one
Among the many there; and while the mists
Flying, and rainy vapours, call out shapes
And phantoms from the crags and solid earth
As fast as a musician scatters sounds
Out of an instrument . . .

WILLIAM WORDSWORTH, 1814

HIGH GAIT TARN AS THE STORM
APPROACHES.

Mists & clouds, & sunshine make endless combinations, as if heaven & Earth were forever talking to each other.

S.T. COLERIDGE

A MAELSTROM OF SNOW AS THE STORM IS UNLEASHED.

O it was a wild business! Such hurry-scurry of Clouds, such volleys of sound!

S.T. COLERIDGE

HIGH GAIT TARN AND ESK BUTTRESS AFTER THE STORM.

SPRING

May 4th, Tuesday. *It was very hot; we were almost melted before we were at the top of the hill. We saw Coleridge on the Wytheburn side of the water; he crossed the beck to us. We came down, and rested upon a moss-covered rock, rising out of the bed of the river. William and C. repeated and read verses. I drank a little brandy and water, and was in Heaven. The stag's horn is very beautiful and fresh, springing upon the fells. Mountain ashes, green.*
DOROTHY WORDSWORTH, 1802

ALL AT ONCE, A HOST OF BLUEBELLS, ABOVE GRASMERE.

DAWN ON THE LANGDALE PIKES IN MARCH . . .

. . . AND TEN WEEKS LATER (BELOW).

(RIGHT) GREAT CARRS FROM ELTERWATER IN WINTER . . .

. . . AND SPRING.

SOURMILK GILL, BUTTERMERE,
IN MAY.

AFTER HEAVY RAIN THE SLABBY
BED OF THE GILL BECOMES A
CATARACT OF A THOUSAND
STREAMS PRODUCING A DEEP,
HYPNOTIC HISSING SOUND LIKE
THE ROAR OF DISTANT SURF.

THE HEAD OF ULLSWATER
AFTER A DAY OF RAIN.

*A drizzling rain. Heavy masses of
shapeless vapour upon the
mountains, yet it is no unbroken
tale of dull sadness. Slanting pillars
travel across the lake at long
intervals, the vaporous mass
whitens in large stains of light –
Little woolpacks of white bright
vapour rest on different summits
and declivities.*

S.T. COLERIDGE, 1803

RAINBOW OVER GLENCOYNE
PARK, ULLSWATER.

RAINBOW OVER ULLSWATER,
FROM GLENCOYNE BROW.

THE SUN COMES OUT. THE
SOUTHERN END OF ULLSWATER
IN THE LATE EVENING.

"How does the Water
Come down at Lodore?"
My little boy ask'd me
Thus, once on a time ...

WATENDLATH TARN.

From its sources which well
In the Tarn on the fell;
From its fountains
In the mountains,
Its rills and its gills;
Through moss and through brake,
It runs and it creeps ...

Through meadow and glade,
In sun and in shade,
And through the wood-shelter,
Among crags in its flurry,
Helter-skelter,
Hurry-scurry.
Here it comes sparkling,
And there it lies darkling;
Now smoaking and frothing
Its tumult and wrath in,
Till in this rapid race
On which it is bent
It reaches the place
Of its steep descent.

WATENDLATH BECK.

The Cataract strong
Then plunges along,
Striking and raging
As if a war waging
Its caverns and rocks among:
Rising and leaping,
Sinking and creeping,
Swelling and sweeping
Showering and springing,
Flying and flinging,
Writhing and ringing,
Eddying and whisking,
Spouting and frisking,
Turning and twisting,
Around and around
With endless rebound!
Smiting and fighting,
A sight to delight in;
Confounding, astounding,
Dizzying and deafening
The ear with its sound.

LODORE FALLS IN FULL SPATE
AFTER DAYS OF RAIN.

. . . And pouring and roaring
And waving and raving,
And tossing and crossing,
And flowing and going.
And running and stunning,
And foaming and roaming,
And dinning and spinning.

And glittering and frittering,
And gathering and feathering,
And whitening and brightening,
And quivering and shivering,
And hurrying and scurrying,
And thundering and floundering . . .

Dividing and gliding and sliding,
And falling and brawling and sprawling,
And driving and riving and striving,
And sprinkling and twinkling and wrinkling,
And sounding and bounding and rounding,
And bubbling and troubling and doubling,
And grumbling and rumbling and tumbling,
And clattering and battering and shattering;

Retreating and beating and meeting and sheeting,
Delaying and straying and playing and spraying,
Advancing and prancing and glancing and dancing,
Recoiling, turmoiling and toiling and boiling,
And gleaming and streaming and steaming and beaming,
And rushing and flushing and brushing and gushing,
And flapping and rapping and clapping and slapping,
And curling and whirling and purling and twirling,
And humping and plumping and bumping and jumping,
And dashing and flashing and splashing and clashing,
And so never ending, but always descending,
Sounds and motions for ever and ever are blending,
All at once and all o'er, with a mighty uproar,
And this way the Water comes down at Lodore.
ROBERT SOUTHEY, *THE CATARACT OF LODORE.*

THE FINAL CATARACT OF THE
LODORE FALLS.

LANDSCAPES OF THE IMAGINATION

*The real majesty of the
appearance of a thing to us
depends upon the degree in which
we ourselves possess the power of
understanding it, – that
penetrating, possession-taking
power of the imagination, which is
the very life of the man,
considered as a* seeing *creature.
Vials that have lain sealed in the
deep sea a thousand years it
unseals, and brings out of them
Genii.*

JOHN RUSKIN, 1856

DERWENT WATER AND SHEPHERDS CRAG FROM BRANDELHOW BAY.

SPRING EVENING, DERWENT
BAY, DERWENT WATER.

(PAGE 114/115) THE SAME
PANORAMA CONTINUED:
DERWENT BAY AND CAT BELLS.

ST HERBERT'S ISLAND FROM
DERWENT BAY, DERWENT
WATER . . .

. . . 'OWL ISLAND' IN BEATRIX
POTTER'S *TALE OF SQUIRREL
NUTKIN*.

THEY made little rafts out of
twigs, and they paddled away
over the water to Owl Island to
gather nuts.

Each Squirrel had a little sack
and a large oar, and spread out his
tail for a sail.

BEATRIX POTTER, *THE TALE
OF SQUIRREL NUTKIN*

Early in the morning, between dark and daylight, Pigling tied up his little bundle and woke up Pigwig. She was excited and half-frightened. "But it's dark! How can we find our way?" . . .

SUNRISE OVER THE RIVER BRATHAY.

. . . The sun rose while they were crossing the moor, a dazzle of light over the tops of the hills . . .

ELTER WATER FROM PARK FELL BEFORE DAWN.

. . . The sunshine crept down the slopes into the peaceful green valleys, where little white cottages nestled in gardens and orchards.

"That's Westmorland," said Pig-wig.

BEATRIX POTTER, *THE TALE OF PIGLING BLAND*

EARLY MORNING ABOVE
COLWITH BRIDGE.

LINGMOOR FELL, LITTLE
LANGDALE, AT DAWN.

'KANCHENJUNGA' AS SEEN
FROM 'DARIEN' IN ARTHUR
RANSOME'S *SWALLOWDALE*:
LOOKING OUT OVER HIGH PEEL
NEAR TO DOW CRAG AND THE
OLD MAN OF CONISTON.

CONISTON WATER AND THE
BLAWITH FELLS.

PEEL ISLAND, CONISTON
WATER, FROM BLAWITH
BEACON.

SURREAL LATE EVENING LIGHT
ABOVE GATE CRAG.

124

THE PRIMEVAL VOLCANIC
LANDSCAPE OF GATE CRAG AND
CROOK CRAG ABOVE ESKDALE.

ESKDALE ON A PERFECT
EVENING IN MAY.

FORESTRY

This great society is going smash;
They cannot fool us with how fast they go,
How much they cost each other and the gods!
A culture is no better than its woods.

W.H. AUDEN, *WINDS*

GILLERTHWAITE AND ENNERDALE FOREST FROM PILLAR IN FEBRUARY.

. . . across the lake you see the tremendous skyline of Pillar, Scoatfell and Steeple, a skyline individual and full of character and unforgettable, one of the three or four most shattering effects in all the district: less known, less written up, and much less often seen than the skyline of the Scafell ridge, or of Bowfell, or of Skiddaw, or the Gable, but unique . . .

REV. H.H. SYMONDS, 1933

PILLAR, SCOAT FELL AND HAYCOCK ACROSS ENNERDALE WATER.

The planting is continuous, by the square mile. What is seen is the rigid and monotonous ranks of spruce, dark green to blackish, goose-stepping on the fell side. Their colour – you must except the larch – is in effect one steady tone all round the dull year: there are no glories of spring and autumn for the conifer. And to the long unbroken mileage of drab, dead colour, you must add the curse of the uniformity in growth.

REV. H.H. SYMONDS, 1936

TREE FELLING ON THE SLOPES
OF HIGH STILE, ENNERDALE.

ENNERDALE FOREST FROM
PILLAR.

STORM DAMAGE IN HIGH PARK
PLANTATION, NEAR
HAWKSHEAD.

Unlike the mountains, which I have always found surprisingly hospitable, these great unnatural forests are decidedly spooky, even in broad daylight. Everywhere there are dead trees and the sounds of death, of the natural order of things being upturned and dying. In the slightest breeze, the trees rattle like skeletons, creaking and groaning. Is it the result of acid rain, or a lack of rain? Or something worse? I don't know. But one thing strikes me forcibly when I look at it: that all this decay and destruction, the acid rain and the hurricanes, is the result of man's messing about with nature. Of man playing God. *And nature will have none of it.*

WASDALE:
HEART OF LAKELAND

There are no hills
Like the Wasdale hills
When spring comes up the dale.
GEORGE BASTERFIELD, 1935

WASTWATER AND GREAT GABLE.

On the approach to
Wastwater.

First sight of the screes
near Woodhow Farm.

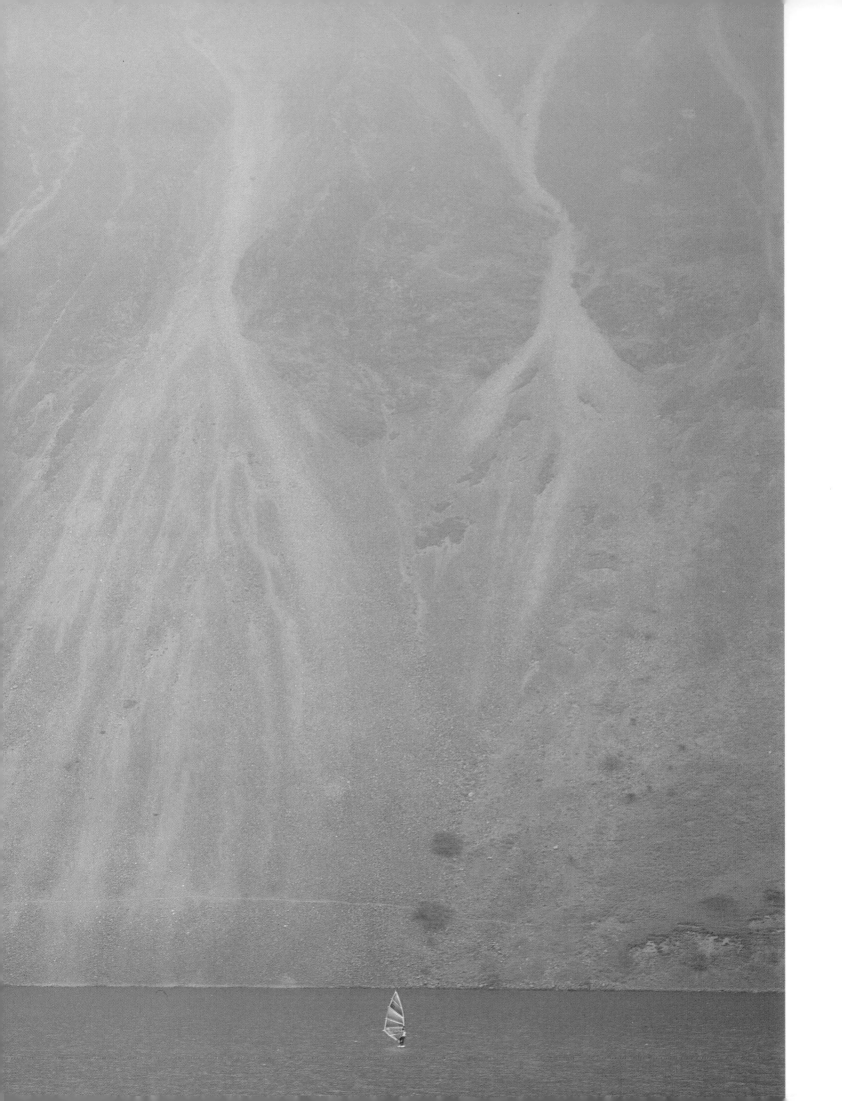

WASTWATER AND GREAT GABLE
FROM LOW WOOD.

A LONE WINDSURFER DWARFED
BY THE WASTWATER SCREES.

WASDALE HEAD HOTEL AND
LINGMELL BECK.

BURNTHWAITE FARM, WHERE
COLERIDGE STAYED THE NIGHT
BEFORE HIS ESCAPADE ON
SCAFELL.

WASTWATER IN A HEAT WAVE.

When people go forth to see the world, they are sometimes in search of beauty. If beauty is the leading object of their search, they need not go to Wast Water. The mountains of Wast Water are naked to their base; their sides and their summits are uniform; their summits shoot up to lofty points. We have heard of the Pyramids of Egypt, built by the hand of man; but these are the Pyramids of the world, built by the Architect of the Universe.

THOMAS WILKINSON, 1824

142

HIGH CAMP AT HOLLOW
STONES, BELOW SCAFELL CRAG.

we lay back
replete as the resting turf
and let night come
to the rattle of beck boulders
and conversation
stilled by flares of shooting stars
entranced by arches of orbit
silent moments of fiery extinction
TERRY GIFFORD, 1991

STARS OVER PIKE'S CRAG FROM
OUR CAMP AT HOLLOW STONES.

MORNING MIST ON BOWFELL.

ON THE SUMMIT OF SCAFELL
PIKE AT DAWN: SUNRISE OVER
ESK PIKE.

SUNRISE ON THE SUMMIT OF
SCAFELL PIKE AT EASTER.

GREAT GABLE FROM SCAFELL
PIKE.

*In all weathers Scafell is king –
lord of the hearts of many who
have climbed his precipices, and
some have given their lives to him;
and of the hearts of those who
walk his ridges and look in wonder
at his glorious and impregnable
beauties; for all who have given
their love to him.*

REV. H.H. SYMONDS, 1933

THE INCOMPARABLE SCAFELL
CRAG ON AN APRIL EVENING.

ON THE UPPER PART OF LORD'S
RAKE, SCAFELL CRAG.

'THE FRIGHTFULLEST COVE
THAT MIGHT EVER BE SEEN . . .'
THE WEST WALL TRAVERSE INTO
DEEP GHYLL, SCAFELL CRAG.

SCAFELL CRAG TOWERS ABOVE
HOLLOW STONES, MIDSUMMER.

*Mighty things have been achieved
upon these bastions, and many a
man grows old with a picture in his
mind, that he conjures up
sometimes by the fireside, of
summer evenings on the Pinnacle.
Everyone has gone home for
dinner, the crag that has been in
shadow all day wakes up and
comes to fresh life as the sun sets
ablaze all the significant detail of
the sound grey rock face that
stretches in a clean sweep upwards
and downwards from his hands
and feet.*

W. HEATON COOPER, 1938

CLIMBERS ON THE KNIFE EDGE
ARETE OF SCAFELL PINNACLE
IN THE EVENING.

In almost all rocks there is a tendency to split transversely in some directions rather than others, giving rise to what geologists call "joints", and throwing the whole rock into blocks more or less rhomboidal ... and giving to all mountains a particular cast and inclination; like the exertion of voluntary power in a definite direction, an internal spirit, manifesting itself in every crag, and breathing in every slope, flinging and forcing the mighty mass towards the heaven with an expression and an energy like that of life.

JOHN RUSKIN, 1843

THE MOST POWERFUL SKYLINE IN ENGLAND: THE LEFT SIDE OF SCAFELL CRAG ON A FINE SUMMER EVENING.

THE TRADITION LIVES ON . . .

As the fiery young earth grows cooler its face settles into maturity. Rain and sun, frost and blazing heat, and the orderly cycle of moisture ascending, moving and falling, smooth and chisel it into shape. Then comes man, with a gift of detached appreciation that grows in him as his physical needs become less urgent. His eyes stray often to the hills, till they become linked up in his mind with the thought of freedom. Alone, on them, he can lose himself in astonishment at the purpose and reason behind the interplay of sky and water and rock, things which obey completely the laws that govern them.

W. HEATON COOPER, 1938

CLIMBER AND ARTIST: JULIAN HEATON COOPER ON GREAT CARRS BUTTRESS.

CLIMBING WRITER, DAVID
CRAIG.

ON NEEDLE RIDGE, GREAT
GABLE, IN THE MIST.

Here every flake and slab and edge is strong as an ancient bell. From the top you look down into chaos – multiple gullies choked with sharp scree barely at the angle of rest, and crests where monoliths balance on gendarmes like henges left by a Bronze Age people. Is it an illusion that this place is in its last few thousand years of integral being and we have arrived only just in time to make something of it? At least, across the way, Scafell Main Face looks good for countless millennia yet.

DAVID CRAIG, 1992

DAVID CRAIG IN HIS ELEMENT ON PIKE'S CRAG, WITH SCAFELL CRAG BEHIND.

163

TERRY GIFFORD LEADING THE
TOP PITCH OF 'THE FANG' ON
GOUTHER CRAG, SWINDALE.

After The Fang, the flow –
after the sudden sharp steepening
of The Fang's final edge,
the sheer flow of limbs
over the rough back
of the creature half hidden
in Swindale's fellside.
TERRY GIFFORD, 1992

TERRY GIFFORD ON 'TRUSS
BUTTRESS', GOUTHER CRAG.

AUTUMN

October 21, 1803

The woody Castle Crag between me and Lodore is a rich flower-garden of colours – the brightest yellows with the deepest crimsons and the infinite shades of brown and green, the infinite *diversity of which blends the whole, so that the brighter colours seem to be colours upon a ground, not coloured things. The vale is narrowed by the mist and cloud, yet through the wall of mist you can see into a bower of sunny light; the birds are singing in the tender rain, as if it were the rain of April, and the decaying foliage were flowers and blossoms.*

S.T. COLERIDGE

NEAR THE BOTTOM OF THE HARD KNOTT PASS, ESKDALE, IN NOVEMBER.

BUTTERMERE AND ROBINSON IN
THE EVENING.

BURTNESS WOOD,
BUTTERMERE.

TARN HOWS ON A GREY DAY IN
NOVEMBER.

TARN HOWS IN THE AUTUMN.
PART OF THE MONK CONISTON
ESTATE WHICH MRS HEELIS
(BEATRIX POTTER) BOUGHT IN
1929 AND THEN SOLD TO THE
NATIONAL TRUST AT COST.

*You found some of England that is
still unspoilt. It is most unfortunate
how much has been wilfully
destroyed in the English country
side. I have tried to do my humble
bit of preservation in this district.*
MRS HEELIS (BEATRIX POTTER),
shortly before her death in 1943.

YEW TREE FARM, YEWDALE –
PART OF BEATRIX POTTER'S
MONK CONISTON ESTATE.

MIDSUMMER SUNRISE

... Magnificent
The morning rose, in memorable pomp,
Glorious as e'er I had beheld – in front,
The sea lay laughing at a distance; near,
The solid mountains shone, bright as the clouds,
Grain-tinctured, drenched in empyrean light ...
WILLIAM WORDSWORTH, 1805

THE VIEW NORTH-EASTWARDS OVER BORROWDALE FROM GREEN GABLE BEFORE DAWN.

LITTLE DID I REALIZE WHEN I WAS LAST HERE, IN THE WINTER, THAT TEN YEARS LATER I WOULD BE SPENDING THE NIGHT OUT AT THIS VERY SPOT, WITH NO FOOD OR SLEEPING BAG, BUT A LOT OF PHOTOGRAPHIC EQUIPMENT.

ENNERDALE AND BUTTERMERE
FROM GREEN GABLE BEFORE
SUNRISE.

SUNRISE OVER BORROWDALE,
FROM GREEN GABLE.

THE EASTERN FELLS AND
LANGDALE PIKES FROM GREAT
GABLE IN THE EARLY MORNING.

NIGHTFALL OVER THE LANGDALE PIKES.

So I continue to doze by the fire,
thinking of what may never come
to pass, and deriving fresh
inspiration by occasional reference
to the outspread map, with its
pregnant network of lines and dots
and thought-quickening names.
L.J. OPPENHEIMER, 1908

Imagination having been our theme,
So also hath that intellectual Love,
For they are each in each, and cannot stand
Dividually. – Here must thou be, O Man!
Power to thyself . . .
WORDSWORTH, *THE PRELUDE, XIV*

The Lake District

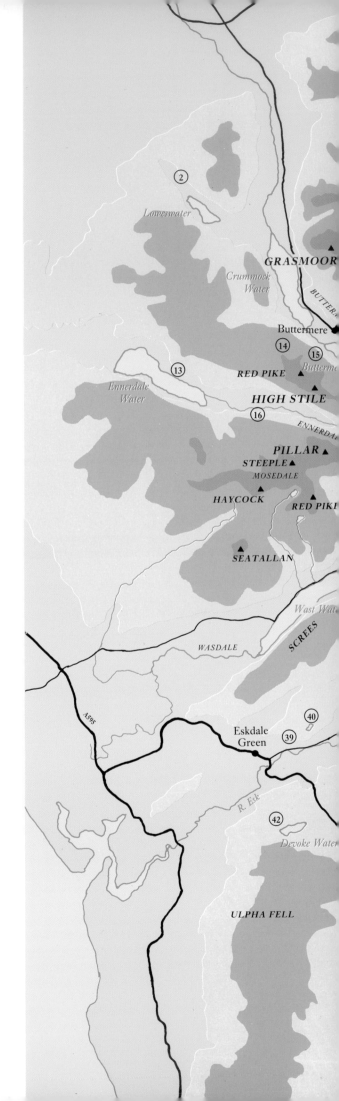

SELECT BIBLIOGRAPHY

ABRAHAM, GEORGE D., *British Mountain Climbs* (London, 1923)

CAMPBELL, JOSEPH, *Creative Mythology* (New York, 1968)

COLERIDGE, SAMUEL TAYLOR, *Anima Poetae* (London, 1895)

COLLINGWOOD, W. G., *The Lake Counties* (London, 1902)

CONWAY, SIR MARTIN, *Mountain Memories* (London, 1920)

DE QUINCEY, THOMAS, *Recollections of the Lakes and the Lake Poets* (London, 1840)

—*Suspiria de Profundis* (Edinburgh, 1845)

EVERSLEY, RUTH, *Wasdale, A Celebration in Words and Pictures* (Beckermet, 1981)

HANKINSON, ALAN, *The First Tigers* (J.M. Dent, 1972)

—*A Century on the Crags* (J.M. Dent, 1988)

—*Coleridge Walks the Fells* (Ellenbank Press, 1991)

HASKETT SMITH, W.. P., *Climbing in the British Isles* (London, 1894)

HEATON COOPER, W., *The Hills of Lakeland* (London, 1938)

HOLMES, RICHARD, *Coleridge, Early Visions* (Hodder & Stoughton, 1989)

OPPENHEIMER, LEHMANN J., *The Heart of Lakeland* (London, 1908)

PILLEY, DOROTHY, *Climbing Days* (London, 1935)

POTTER, BEATRIX, *The Tale of Squirrel Nutkin* (Frederick Warne, 1903)

—*The Tale of Pigling Bland* (Frederick Warne, 1913)

RUSKIN, JOHN, *Modern Painters* (London 1843–1860)

—*The Ethics of the Dust* (London, 1865)

—*The Queen of the Air* (London, 1869)

STAINFORTH, GORDON, *Eyes to the Hills* (Constable, 1991)

SYMONDS, H., H., *Walking in the Lake District* (London, 1933)

—*Afforestation in the Lake District* (London, 1936)

TAYLOR, WHALLEY, HOBBS, BATTRICK, *Beatrix Potter, The Artist and her World* (Frederick Warne/National Trust, 1987)

THOREAU, HENRY DAVID, *Walking* (Boston, 1862)

ACKNOWLEDGEMENTS

I am indebted to the following for their help, which ranged all the way from useful advice to spending long days out with me on the hill:

Neil Allinson, the Upland Access Advisor of the National Trust; Julian and Linda Heaton Cooper; David Craig; Hazel Davidson of the Keswick Museum and Art Gallery for providing crystals from the museum collection for use in my introduction (p.12); David Dunk; Norman Elliott; Fuji film for providing most of the film stock for the 1992 shoot; Terry Gifford for permission to use the poem 'Deepdale Camp' from his book 'Outcrops' and also for supplying new poetry at the drop of a hat; Tony Greenbank; David Hope; Zbigniew Kotowicz for assisting me on two high mountain camps on Scafell and for general intellectual stimulation; Miss Dymock of the Lingholm Estate for access to Derwent Bay, Derwent Water; Bob and Barbara McGovern; Tim and Liz Melling of Nab Cottage, Rydal; John Mitchell for the map; Nic Pancisi of Multiprint Laboratories, Derby, for the film processing; Guy and Val Richardson for their wonderful hospitality and general assistance, and Guy for the use of his map illustrated on p.21; Jon and Jackie Rigby; David Rose; Anthony, Christine, and Colin Harrison of the Smallwood House Hotel, Ambleside; and Frederick Warne for permission to reproduce three illustrations from the works of Beatrix Potter.

All the photographs (except for two
35mm shots) were taken on a Hasselblad
500 C/M 6 × 6 cm roll film SLR camera

FILM STOCKS
RFP Fujichrome 50D Professional 120
RDP Fujichrome 100D Professional 120
RVP Fujichrome Velvia 120 (50 ISO)
EPR Ektachrome 64 Professional 120
EPN Ektachrome 100 Professional 120
EPP Ektachrome 100 Plus Prof 120
EPX Ektachrome 64X Professional 120
EPZ Ektachrome 100X Professional 120
KR Kodachrome 64 135

LENSES
50mm Zeiss Distagon CF 500mm F4
80mm Zeiss Planar CF 80mm F2.8
150mm Zeiss Sonnar CF 150mm F4
TC   Teleplus MC6 2 × Teleconvertor

× 2   Montage of two frames

FILTERS
SL Skylight or 1A filter
UV Ultraviolet filter
81A 81A (light amber) filter
G1 Graduated ND filter – 1 stop
G2 Graduated ND filter – 2 stops
POL Polarizer

No.	Title	Time	Season	Lens	Aperture	Speed	Filter	Film
Cover	Elter Water and the Langdale Pikes.	7.45 a.m.	Mid-May	80mm	f6.8	1/125	SL	RVP
1	Glencoyne Brow, Ullswater.	5.50 p.m.	Early June	50mm	f6.8	1/125	UV	RDP
2/3	Langdale at sunset.	9.15 p.m.	Late May	150mm	f6.8	1/60	81A	RDP
4/5	Scafells from the head of Mosedale.	1.15 p.m.	Late March	150mm	f9.5	1/250	81A	EPX
6	Across Crinkle Crags.	4.20 p.m.	Late April	80mm	f11	1/250	SL	RDP
10	Hard Tarn, Ruthwaite Cove.	2.30 p.m.	Late May	50mm	f16	1/60	UV	EPR
14	Lightweight tent, Great Moss.	10.00 a.m.	Late March	150mm	f4.7	1/250	81A	EPR
15	Hell Gill, Langdale.	6.30 p.m.	Early June	150mm	f4.7	1/125	81A	RDP
16	Pitched footpath, Dungeon Ghyll.	5.30 p.m.	Late May	80mm	f6.8	1/60	SL	RFP
19	Central Buttress, Scafell Crag.	4.25 p.m.	Early June	150mm + TC	f4	1/60	81A	RDP
26	A peaceful evening in Grisedale.	7.00 p.m.	Late May	80mm	f6.8	1/125	SL	EPR
28	Helvellyn from Black Fell.	6.25 p.m.	Early April	150mm	f8	1/125	81A	RDP
29	Rydal Water, early morning.	6.45 a.m.	Mid-May	50mm	f8	1/125	UV	RDP
30	Birch trees on King's How.	6.40 p.m.	Mid-May	50mm	f6.8	1/250	UV	RDP
31	Descending into Troutdale.	5.45 p.m.	Mid-May	80mm	f5.6	1/250	SL	RVP
32	Troutdale and Black Crag.	6.40 p.m.	Mid-May	50mm	f6.8	1/250	UV	RDP
33	Borrowdale from Maiden Moor.	4.15 p.m.	Mid-May	80mm	f8	1/250	G1	EPX
34	Thirlmere from Launchy Gill.	2.25 p.m.	Late April	80mm	f8	1/250	SL	RDP
35	Ennerdale Water, late afternoon.	6.15 p.m.	Mid-May	150mm	f4	1/125	POL	EPX
36	Styhead Tarn, late evening.	9.30 p.m.	Early June	150mm	f4.7	1/60	81A	RDP
37	Late snow on Stony Cove Pike.	12.50 p.m.	Mid-March	80mm	f11	1/250	SL	RVP
38	Lichen on Cat Bells, Borrowdale.	5.30 p.m.	Mid-May	80mm	f8	1/15	SL	EPX
40	Quartz-topaz on Water Crag.	5.40 p.m.	Late April	80mm	f9.5	1/125	SL	RDP
41	Summit boulder on Lingmell.	4.40 p.m.	Late April	80mm	f8	1/250	SL	RDP
42	Outcrop on Maiden Moor.	4.30 p.m.	Mid-May	80mm	f8	1/250	SL	EPX
43	'Painted wall', Castle Crag.	4.10 p.m.	Mid-May	80mm	f13.5	1/8	SL	RDP
44	Cave ceiling, Castle Crag.	1.00 p.m.	Early May	80mm	f4	1/8	SL	EPX
45	'Painted wall', Castle Crag.	4.10 p.m.	Mid-May	80mm	f9.5	1/8	SL	RDP
46	Natural tear on the 'painted wall'.	4.10 p.m.	Mid-May	80mm	f9.5	1/8	SL	RDP
47	Gorse on Cat Bells, Borrowdale.	5.20 p.m.	Mid-May	80mm	f4	1/60	SL	EPX
48	The Scafell Pikes from Grey Friar.	10.00 a.m.	Late March	150mm	f6.8	1/500	81A	EPX
50	The upper end of Deepdale.	12.50 p.m.	Early April	80mm	f8	1/125	SL	RDP
51	Pike of Stickle from Flat Crags.	4.00 p.m.	Late April	80mm	f8	1/250	SL	RDP
52	Eskdale Fell and Esk Pike, evening.	7.05 p.m.	Mid-May	150mm	f6.8	1/125	POL	RDP
53	Across Blind Tarn to Ulpha Fell.	8.15 p.m.	Mid-May	150mm	f4	1/250	81A	RDP
54	Blea Tarn, Eskdale.	8.10 p.m.	Mid-May	150mm	f8	1/125	81A	RDP
55	The Irish Sea from Blea Tarn.	8.40 p.m.	Mid-May	50mm	f6.8	1/60	UV	RDP
56	The Great Gully, Wastwater Screes.	2.15 p.m.	Mid-May	150mm	f5.6	1/250	81A	RVP
57	Scale Force.	2.55 p.m.	Late April	50mm	f6.8	1/15	UV	EPZ
58	East face of Ill Crag, Scafell Pike.	11.15 a.m.	Late March	50mm	f19	1/125	G2	EPR
60/1	St Sunday Crag and Deepdale.	3.45 p.m.	Early April	50mm × 2	f16	1/250	UV	RDP
62	Cairn on Caudale Moor in winter.	1.15 p.m.	Mid-February	50mm	f8	1/250	UV	RVP

63	Icy boulders above Kirkstone Pass.	1.30 p.m.	Mid-February	50mm	f11	1/250	UV	RVP
64	On the Kirkstone Road before dawn.	6.30 a.m.	Mid-March	50mm	f4	1/30	UV	RDP
65	The same, at dawn.	6.40 a.m.	Mid-March	50mm	f4.7	1/60	UV	RDP
66	Across Dovedale to Helvellyn.	11.20 a.m.	Mid-March	150mm	f13.5	1/500	81A	RDP
67	The eastern coves of Helvellyn.	1.10 p.m.	Early April	150mm	f13.5	1/250	81A	RFP
68	Helvellyn from Fairfield in winter.	2.55 p.m.	Early April	150mm	f11	1/500	81A	RDP
69	Grisedale Tarn.	1.10 p.m.	Early April	80mm	f8	1/500	SL	RFP
70	Dollywaggon Pike in winter.	1.35 p.m.	Early April	150mm	f8	1/250	81A	RFP
71	On Great Gable in winter.	2.00 p.m.	Late November	35mm (Olympus XA2)				KR
72/3	Sharp Edge, Blencathra.	2.15 p.m.	Early April	150mm × 2	f6.8	1/500	81A	RDP
74/5	High on Grasmoor in February.	5.15 p.m.	Mid-February	80mm	f2.8	1/30	SL	RVP
76	Scafell Pike from head of Mosedale.	12.55 p.m.	Late March	150mm	f9.5	1/250	81A	RFP
78/9	The Scafell Pikes from Great Moss.	8.30 a.m.	Late March	50mm	f8	1/125	UV	EPR
80	Scafell Pike from Great Moss.	8.15 a.m.	Late March	150mm	f5.6	1/250	81A	EPR
81	Mickledore and Cam Spout.	3.15 p.m.	Late March	150mm	f8	1/250	81A	EPR
82/3	Camping in Upper Eskdale, March.	9.00 a.m.	Late March	80mm × 2	f6.8	1/250	SL	EPR
84	High Gait Crags before a storm.	2.30 p.m.	Late March	80mm	f8	1/500	SL	RDP
85	Ominous clouds gather over Scafell.	5.45 p.m.	Late March	50mm	f4.7	1/125	UV	EPR
87	High Gait Tarn, storm gathering.	3.10 p.m.	Late March	50mm	f13.5	1/250	UV	RDP
88	A maelstrom of snow.	3.00 p.m.	Late March	50mm	f11	1/125	UV	RDP
89	High Gait Tarn after the storm.	3.25 p.m.	Late March	50mm	f6.8	1/250	UV	RDP
90	Bluebells above Grasmere.	6.50 p.m.	Early May	80mm	f9.5	1/60	G1	EPX
92	Dawn on Langdale Pikes, winter …	7.40 a.m.	Mid-March	150mm + TC	f4	1/60	81A	RVP
92	… and ten weeks later.	6.50 a.m.	Late May	150mm + TC	f4.7	1/125	81A	RDP
93	Great Carrs from Elterwater, winter.	7.50 a.m.	Mid-March	150mm + TC	f4.7	1/60	81A	RDP
93	… and spring.	7.00 a.m.	Late May	150mm + TC	f5.6	1/125	81A	RDP
94	Sourmilk Gill, Buttermere.	8.15 p.m.	Late May	150mm	f4.7	1/60	POL	EPN
95	Sourmilk Gill after heavy rain.	7.05 p.m.	Late April	80mm	f4	1/125	SL	EPN
96	The head of Ullswater after rain.	6.45 p.m.	Early June	50mm	f6.8	1/125	UV	RDP
97	Rainbow over Glencoyne Park.	6.45 p.m.	Early June	50mm	f8	1/125	UV	RDP
99	Rainbow over Ullswater.	5.45 p.m.	Early June	80mm	f6.8	1/125	SL	RDP
100/1	Southern end of Ullswater, evening.	7.50 p.m.	Early June	80mm	f11	1/30	SL	RDP
102	Watendlath Tarn.	3.50 p.m.	Mid-May	50mm	f9.5	1/125	UV	RVP
103	Watendlath Beck.	3.10 p.m.	Mid-May	150mm	f5.6	1/125	81A	RVP
103	Watendlath Beck.	1.25 p.m.	Mid-May	80mm	f9.5	1/60	SL	RVP
104	Lodore Falls.	2.20 p.m.	Mid-May	50mm	f8	1/125	UV	RVP
105	Lodore Falls.	12.55 p.m.	Mid-May	80mm	f13.5	1/125	SL	RDP
106	Lodore Falls.	1.50 p.m.	Mid-May	80mm	f5.6	1/250	SL	EPX
106	Lodore Falls.	2.05 p.m.	Mid-May	80mm	f8	1/125	SL	EPX
107	Lodore Falls.	1.20 p.m.	Mid-May	150mm	f13.5	1/15	81A	EPX
109	Final cataract of the Lodore Falls.	12.15 p.m.	Mid-May	150mm	f16	1/125	81A	RDP
110	Brandelhow Bay, Derwent Water.	4.00 p.m.	Mid-May	150mm	f4	1/125	POL	RFP
112/3	Spring evening, Derwent Water.	7.15 p.m.	Mid-May	150mm × 2	f6.8	1/60	POL	RDP
114/5	Derwent Bay and Cat Bells.	7.05 p.m.	Mid-May	150mm × 2	f4.7	1/60	POL	RVP
116	St Herbert's Island.	1.35 p.m.	Mid-May	80mm	f22	1/4	POL	RFP
118	Elter Water before dawn.	5.30 a.m.	Mid-May	50mm	f4	1/60	UV	RVP
119	Sunrise over the River Brathay.	5.35 a.m.	Mid-May	150mm	f4.7	1/125	81A	RVP
120	Lingmoor Fell at dawn.	6.25 a.m.	Mid-May	80mm	f5.6	1/60	SL	RFP
121	Early morning near Colwith Bridge.	6.55 a.m.	Mid-May	80mm	f4	1/250	SL	RFP
122	Coniston Water and Blawith Fells.	8.30 a.m.	Mid-May	150mm	f6.8	1/125	POL	RDP
122	Peel Island, Coniston Water.	10.45 a.m.	Mid-May	80mm	f9.5	1/30	POL	RVP
123	Dow Crag and Old Man of Coniston.	8.40 a.m.	Mid-May	150mm	f8	1/60	POL	RFP
124	Gate Crag, Eskdale.	7.30 p.m.	Mid-May	150mm	f9.5	1/125	81A	RDP

125	Late evening above Gate Crag.	8.30 p.m.	Mid-May	80mm	f5.6	1/125	SL	RDP
126/7	Eskdale on a perfect evening.	6.30 p.m.	Mid-May	80mm × 2	f9.5	1/125	SL	EPX
128	Gillerthwaite and Ennerdale Forest.	1.25 p.m.	Mid-February	150mm	f8	1/250	81A	EPP
130/1	Pillar group across Ennerdale Water.	6.00 p.m.	Mid-May	80mm × 2	f9.5	1/30	POL	EPX
132	Ennerdale Forest from Pillar.	2.00 p.m.	Mid-February	150mm	f8	1/125	81A	EPP
133	Tree felling, Ennerdale.	1.55 p.m.	Mid-February	150mm	f8	1/125	81A	EPP
134	Forestry storm damage.	1.30 p.m.	Early June	50mm	f9.5	1/30	UV	EPX
134	Forestry storm damage.	2.00 p.m.	Early June	80mm	f13.5	1/15	SL	EPX
135	Forestry storm damage.	1.00 p.m.	Early June	50mm	f5.6	1/60	UV	EPX
136	Wastwater and Great Gable.	4.00 p.m.	Mid-May	80mm	f13.5	1/60	SL	RVP
138	On the approach to Wastwater.	10.45 a.m.	Late June	80mm	f11	1/125	SL	EPN
139	First sight of the Screes.	11.50 a.m.	Mid-May	150mm	f5.6	1/125	81A	RFP
140	A lone windsurfer on Wastwater.	11.35 a.m.	Late June	150mm	f6.8	1/60	81A	EPN
141	Wastwater from Low Wood.	1.45 p.m.	Mid-May	150mm	f9.5	1/60	POL	EPX
142	Wasdale Head Hotel.	11.35 a.m.	Late April	80mm	f9.5	1/250	SL	RDP
142	Burnthwaite Farm, Wasdale.	12.10 p.m.	Late April	150mm + TC	f4	1/250	81A	RDP
143	Wastwater in a heat wave.	12.25 p.m.	Mid-May	50mm	f11	1/60	UV	RFP
144	High camp below Scafell Crag.	10.15 a.m.	Early April	50mm	f8	1/125	UV	EPR
145	Stars over Pike's Crag.	12.45 a.m.	Early April	80mm	f4	7 mins	SL	EPR
146	Sunrise from Scafell Pike.	7.05 a.m.	Early April	150mm	f6.8	1/125	81A	EPR
147	Morning mist on Bowfell.	7.40 a.m.	Early April	150mm	f11	1/125	81A	EPR
148/9	Sunrise on summit of Scafell Pike.	7.20 a.m.	Early April	50mm	f8	1/125	UV	EPR
150	Great Gable from Scafell Pike.	8.30 a.m.	Early April	150mm	f8	1/250	81A	EPR
153	Scafell Crag on a spring evening.	7.00 p.m.	Early April	80mm	f8	1/60	SL	EPR
154	Lord's Rake, Scafell Crag.	2.10 p.m.	Early April	80mm	f6.8	1/125	SL	EPR
155	West Wall Traverse, Scafell Crag.	2.30 p.m.	Early April	80mm	f4.7	1/125	SL	EPR
156	Scafell Crag above Hollow Stones.	3.00 p.m.	Early June	150mm	f8	1/250	81A	RDP
157	Climbers on the Knife-Edge arête.	6.35 p.m.	Early June	80mm	f5.6	1/250	SL	RDP
159	The left side of Scafell Crag.	8.35 p.m.	Early June	150mm	f5.6	1/125	81A	RDP
160	Julian Cooper on Great Carrs.	2.30 p.m.	Early May	80mm	f8	1/250	SL	EPX
162	David Craig.	4.30 p.m.	Early June	80mm	f6.8	1/125	SL	RDP
162	On Needle Ridge, Great Gable.	3.15 p.m.	Late August	50mm	f8	1/125	UV	EPN
163	David Craig on Pike's Crag.	5.00 p.m.	Early June	80mm	f6.8	1/60	SL	RDP
164	Terry Gifford on The Fang.	1.50 p.m.	Early May	150mm	f5.6	1/250	81A	EPX
165	Terry Gifford on Truss Buttress.	3.05 p.m.	Early May	50mm	f6.8	1/250	UV	EPX
166	Eskdale in autumn.	2.15 p.m.	Early November	150mm	f4.7	1/250	SL	EPR
168	Buttermere and Robinson.	6.45 p.m.	Mid-October	80mm	f5.6	1/60	SL	EPN
169	Burtness Wood, Buttermere.	6.50 p.m.	Mid-October	80mm	f4.7	1/60	SL	EPN
170/1	Tarn Hows in November murk.	11.30 a.m.	Early November	150mm	f4.7	1/30	G1	EPR
172	Tarn Hows in the autumn.	12.30 p.m.	Mid-November	50mm	f8	1/125	G2	EPR
173	Tarn Hows in the autumn.	1.00 p.m.	Mid-November	150mm	f5.6	1/125	81A	EPR
174	Yew Tree Farm, Yewdale.	1.30 p.m.	Mid-November	80mm	f5.6	1/125	SL	EPN
176	North-eastwards from Green Gable.	4.30 a.m.	Early June	80mm	f4.7	1/30	SL	RDP
178/9	Ennerdale from Green Gable.	4.35 a.m.	Early June	80mm × 2	f13.5	1/2	SL	RDP
178	The same in the winter.	12.45 p.m.	Late November	35mm (Olympus XA2)				KR
180/1	Sunrise from Green Gable.	5.00 a.m.	Early June	80mm × 2	f13.5	1/15	SL	RVP
182/3	The Eastern Fells from Great Gable.	7.30 a.m.	Early June	80mm × 2	f16	1/250	SL	RDP
184	Nightfall over the Langdale Pikes.	9.20 p.m.	Late May	150mm	f4.7	1/60	81A	RDP
Back cover	Distant Styhead Tarn, late evening	9.25 p.m.	Early June	80mm	f4.7	1/60	SL	RDP